BRITAIN IN

WIGTON & THE SOLWAY PLAIN

ELIZABETH NELSON

ALAN SUTTON PUBLISHING LIMITED

Alan Sutton Publishing Limited
Phoenix Mill · Far Thrupp · Stroud
Gloucestershire · GL5 2BU

First published 1995

Copyright © Elizabeth Nelson, 1995

Cover photograph: (front) Thomas
McMechan's shop, 1911; (back) a new lorry,
c. 1928.

British Library Cataloguing in Publication Data.
A catalogue record for this book is available from
the British Library.

ISBN 0-7509-0851-3

Typeset in 9/10 Sabon.
Typesetting and origination by
Alan Sutton Publishing Limited.
Printed in Great Britain by
Ebenezer Baylis, Worcester.

Contents

A three-masted ship berthed in Silloth New Dock, *c.* 1912.

Introduction

The more secluded corners of the Solway Plain, which can still be found away from main roads, are a haven of tranquillity where it is difficult to imagine the turmoil and strife with which the area has been beset over the centuries. Garrisons of Roman soldiers were stationed on the plain at the western end of Hadrian's Wall to protect against Pictish hordes and, although the wall ended at Bowness-on-Solway, defences carried on right down the coast, for the Solway was quite navigable by boat. No signs of the Roman habitation are visible today west of Carlisle, except for the many Roman stones to be seen in churches and older buildings – the Romans left a ready-made quarry behind them.

Border warfare continued for many centuries, and on its wind-swept marshes, a King of England (the Hammer of the Scots, as Edward I was known) died on his way to wage war on the Scots. There were a number of places where the narrowing estuary could be forded, as the cattle rustlers well knew on their illicit trips over the Border. With the swift ebbing and flowing of the tide, the ever-changing channels and the dangerous sands, one would need to have a knowledge which probably only the expert haaf-net fishermen possess to risk walking across today.

Bounded by water on two sides, it was natural that seamanship should be an established part of the way of life, but the early port of Grune – north of Silloth – had been washed into the sea. Then Port Carlisle became quite a flourishing port, with the canal to take ships right up to Carlisle, but the building of the Solway Viaduct stopped traffic higher up the estuary. The need for a new port was evident and, as ships from further down the coast used to make for off-Silloth – noted for its safe anchorage – in a storm, it was the obvious place for a port.

The coming of the railways meant that ordinary people were within reach of a seaside holiday resort, so Silloth – and to a slightly lesser extent Port Carlisle – became exceedingly popular and crowded throughout the season. Allonby too filled up with visitors, but it was considered the seaside resort of the nobility. With world travel becoming commonplace, the Solway mostly attracts only day visitors now, although the two large holiday camps at Silloth and a number of caravan sites in the area are in great demand. Silloth has had its famous residents, including Cecil Leitch, who must have learned her first strokes on its renowned golf course, and Kathleen Ferrier, whose wonderful voice was discovered when from her home there she entered Carlisle Musical Festival. The invigorating air and the glories of the Solway sunsets add charm to the area.

In a very fertile arable area, Wigton was the natural centre for the market town. For well over 700 years the market has been held there every Tuesday, although, as in most towns today, markets are a very low-key affair compared to what they used to be in the days when farmers' wives were dependent on the weekly market sales of their produce to provide their often meagre living. Many historic buildings have been demolished, but there are still delightful corners and the recent building of a bypass on the northern side has, to some extent, relieved the flow of traffic in the town. The tendency for shoppers to go further afield for larger supermarkets has been slightly obviated by the establishment of ones in the town, while the extensive works of British Rayophane (Overseas) Ltd in the centre of the town has filled gaps caused by the closure of small light industries. An excellent theatre company and a good choir, together with other amenities and the determination of today's residents, are all working to ensure that Wigton will once again become the central point in the Solway Plain.

Approaching the plain from the south – with Lakeland as a backdrop – the view is magnificent, the glistening water of the Solway on the left, with the Scottish coastline stretching away in the distance and, as the water narrows, Criffel standing as a sentinel. Ahead, villages and landmarks can be located in the vastness of the land below and beyond, like a winding silver ribbon, the water of the Firth wends its way until it disappears at the mouths of the rivers that run into it. Further to the right the Pennines rise, forming a natural barrier to this plain, lying as it does surrounded by either hills or sea.

The pele towers of the churches at Burgh-by-Sands and Newton Arlosh are a permanent reminder of the dangers of the border raiders in years gone by, but all such excursions these days are of friendship and goodwill. During the Second World War, forces abounded on the plain, with a number of Royal Air Force Stations and the Royal Naval Air Station at Anthorn, the secluded corner of the country, proving invaluable for flying training. Now all is peaceful, and the RSPB are able to develop their land on both sides of the water for bird havens, with eager 'twitchers' watching the first arrivals each year. The lower fells provide excellent walking for those who do not want to hill-climb, while the delights of Caldbeck and other fell-side villages are a happy refuge from the overcrowded Lake District.

Across the water near Annan, visible from so many directions, are the steaming cooling towers of Chapel Cross nuclear power station, a reminder that, however much we are steeped in history, we cannot escape from the future. Each generation has played a part in shaping this corner of England – may these photographs preserve for future generations something of their heritage.

WIGTON

William James Wallas, known as 'Blin Billt', at
Wigton station in the 1890s, where he regularly
sold sweets and lemonade. Being blind, he was
guided to the site by a small boy. He retired a few
years before he died on 27 April 1910, aged
seventy, in George Street, having lived on the few
savings from this trade.

The staff of Wigton post office at 6 King Street, 1880. The post office has now moved to the High Street, and the King Street premises have become Barclays Bank.

Looking expectantly for customers at the draper's shop in West Street, Wigton. Penrice's moved to these premises from the High Street in 1894. Sadly, this long established firm closed in 1989.

Shoppers are drawn to Penrice's attractively decorated premises in West Street, to celebrate the coronation in 1953.

J. Gate, stationer, King Street, Wigton, published the *History and Topography of Wigton* in 1894. The shop was formerly owned by William Henry Hoodless, who was born in 1841 and was a Wigton artist. Since 1980 the premises have been used as Birkett's bakery.

Wigton Volunteer Band, Water Street, 1865.

Wigton Show, 1908. The show was held each September on the Highmore Estate.

Girls of Wigton National School in their playground. The school, pictured in the background, was in High Street and opened in 1829. The boys were downstairs and the girls upstairs, in what were virtually two schools in the same building, each with a separate playground.

Celebrations at the Throstle's west bowling green, possibly for the coronation of King Edward VII in 1902. The green was behind the Highland Laddie public house in High Street, the site now being occupied by Water Street and the Stocksman restaurant.

John Percival's railway trucks in the goods yard at Wigton station, 1920s.

Percival's dressed horses at Hope's auction mart, *c.* 1915. The old sheep ring is visible in the background on the right-hand side.

The shops of H. Wallace, shoe maker, 22 King Street, and J.K. Jackson, grocer, 20 King Street, *c.* 1900. The shop of H. Wallace is now empty, and that of J.K. Jackson is a fish and chip shop. The arch on the right leads into Church Street, which has become the car park.

Thomas McMechan's shop, King Street, splendidly decorated for the coronation of King George V and Queen Mary in 1911. Thomas McMechan was the founder of the *Wigton Advertiser* newspaper, which ran until 1940, and was a bookseller and publisher. He knew John Peel, the famous huntsman, and John Woodcock Graves, who wrote 'D'ye Ken John Peel', and was involved in numerous organizations.

The premises of Redmayne's, 'The Cumberland Taylors', with bunting out to welcome a visit by Her Majesty the Queen in 1959. Unfortunately, the Queen was ill and Prince Philip came alone.

In 1923 Wigton enjoyed its first carnival after the First World War. Here the procession passes up High Street into the Cornmarket, the photo presumably taken from the Crown and Mitre, which has now gone.

Wigton public park, on land off West Road, was opened in 1924. Here George Johnston JP is speaking at the opening of the bower in the park in 1924. His son still runs the family shoe shop in King Street.

The yard of the Technical Institute, c. 1880. The yard, which used to be at the rear of the Blue Bell inn on Station Road, provides the car park of that day for traps and carts. Until recently this was the site of Wigton bus station.

Lieutenant Colonel C.H. Walker MC, of the Border Regiment, takes the salute as a military parade marches along High Street, Wigton, in 1942. Here the National Fire Service are passing the saluting base.

The Lonsdale battalion of the Border regiment march through High Street on a recruiting drive in 1915. Wigton lost 120 people, including a nurse, in the First World War.

Tommy Millar is undeterred by the floods in Station Road, as the horse pulls him and his fellow travellers through dry-shod. It was not uncommon for flooding to occur here in the 1920s.

'Thacky Hoose', King Street, *c.* 1880. This was a 'jerry shop', licensed to sell ale but not spirits. It is now the site of the former bus station and Throstle's Nest inn.

A steamroller comes into Wigton on the main road from the east and slowly makes its way towards the town centre, *c.* 1912. St Cuthbert's Roman Catholic church can be seen in the centre behind it.

Wigton Carnival, 1937. The float from the Carr White and Co. jam factory shows how jam is made.

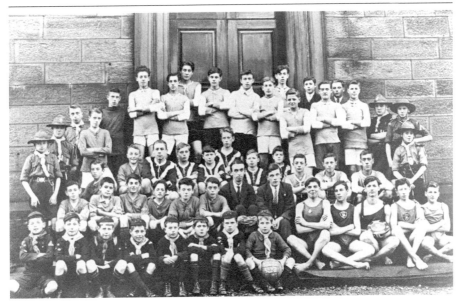

Wigton Boys Club, 1921–2.

Busy at work in Pringle's wood yard, Water Street, 1920s.

King Street, looking east, *c.* 1930. The building jutting out in the middle distance on the left is the Blue Bell Inn – now demolished – on Station Road. The building on the far right, now Barclays Bank, was then the post office.

A typical market day in High Street, before the First World War. One of the four gas lamps surrounding the fountain is just visible on the right-hand corner. The King's Head inn, also on the right and built in the fifteenth century, is reputed to be the oldest building in the town. The overhanging balcony has now been demolished, and the building is a Chinese takeaway.

The George Moore memorial fountain was unveiled on 21 March 1873, in memory of Moore's first wife, Elizabeth, a bust of her being on each side above four bronzes by the pre-Raphaelite sculptor Thomas Woolner. In 1262 Henry III granted Wigton permission to hold a market every Tuesday, and this site in front of the fountain is now designated a fish market. A wet-fish van still parks every Tuesday where this stall is.

Wigton pump and lamp, c. 1860. Unfortunately, the pump often ran dry much to the disgust of Wigtonians as it was one of the few water pumps in the town. The pump was replaced in 1872 during the building of the George Moore memorial fountain. Both the pump and lamp can be found today in Wigton Park.

David Lyndon Powell, manager (right), and Bobby Bell, barman, stand outside the Spirit Vaults inn, 33 King Street, 1910. This is now the O'Calcutta Restaurant. On the right of the picture can be seen the entrance to the old post office.

The Corn Market, High Street, *c.* 1915. No one is afraid of traffic, and conversations take place all over the street regardless of the horse droppings, a result of the transport of the day.

J. Simpson, saddler, West Street, and his staff display their wares.

The Salvation Army harvest festival in Wigton, early twentieth century. This picture might have been taken at the Salvation Army temple in Station Road, now the site of Wigton theatre club.

The devastation after the fire at Hartley's wood yard, Station Road, 6 September 1915.

St Mary's Church, Corn Market, built in 1788 on the site of Odard's church of the early twelfth century, Odard de Logis being Wigton's first lord of the manor. The gravestones have now been laid flat, while the carts in the foreground stand on what was the Cornmarket. Here the letters 'w' for wheat, 'b' for barley and 'o' for oats can still be seen picked out in white cobbles.

The interior of St Mary's Church, 1922. The gallery is supported on Tuscan order columns, the pillars from gallery to roof are in Doric style and the chancel and sanctuary are in Ionic style. The contractors had made it a condition in 1788 that nothing from the old church was to go into the new one.

The Black-A-Moor's Head inn, a clay daub inn facing Market Hill. Jane Holliday, the last landlady, is seen standing at the door. The inn was demolished in 1893. A new inn, the Black-A-Moor, was built on the site and is open today. Stanley Bragg was the landlord in the 1940s, and his well-known broadcaster and author son Melvyn (born 1939) spent much of his boyhood at the new Black-A-Moor.

The Crown & Mitre inn, Corn Market, 1900s. To the right of the front door can be seen the ring and chain used by customers to tie up their horses. The inn was demolished in the 1970s and Lindsay House shops are now on the site.

Lord Sanger and Son's circus visited Wigton regularly before the First World War. A popular attraction was for local men to try and score a goal past the elephant goalkeeper. Another story is of the elephant which escaped during the night to gorge itself at the Lion and Lamb grain store!

Wigton Hall, West Street, built in the fifteenth century but greatly improved and enlarged in the Gothic style in 1801 by the Revd Richard Matthews. Here can be seen the Kentish sisters, who lived in the Hall from 1882 to 1919.

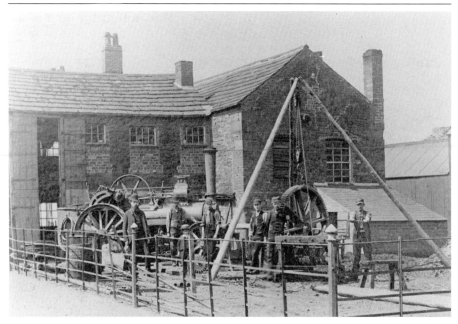

The works of John Hall, engineer and agricultural implement dealer, in Station Road, possibly behind Bloomfield Terrace. John Hall was also described as an inventor of an automatic clock gun for scaring birds.

The drawing-room of Highmoor, the mansion on the southern side of Wigton, *c.* 1880. Built in about 1810, it was at this time owned by the Banks brothers, Henry and Edwin, who travelled extensively abroad, particularly to Italy. The typically Victorian drawing-room shows some of the ornaments and pictures bought on their travels.

A garden party at Highmoor, *c.* 1920. Tea is being enjoyed in the sunshine on the front lawn. The owner at this time was the Hon. Gilbert de St Croix, Henry Banks having died suddenly in 1891, and Edwin Banks being forced to sell the estate and contents of the mansion in 1908.

The Nelson School, built as an up-to-date grammar school, which opened in 1899, with money left by Joseph Nelson of Moor Row, near Wigton. Nelson was a wealthy businessman, who died in June 1895. The first headmaster was the Revd W.E. Humphreys and, by 1920, there was an average attendance of 100 pupils.

The Friends' School was founded at Wigton in 1815 and opened at Highmoor on 4 September of that year with nine boys and eight girls. Needing more accommodation, five acres of land were bought at Brookfield for £520 in 1825. The new school, shown here, was built and the pupils moved in in November 1826.

One of the classrooms at Brookfield. The school was closed in 1985 and bought by the owner of Lime House School, Dalston, to convert into flats. Unfortunately, the building was completely gutted by fire on 30 January 1989.

Section Two

RISING UP TO THE
FELLS

South from Wigton the road rises steadily up Warnell Fell, with panoramic views of the
Solway Plain behind, until it drops down steeply into the attractive village of Caldbeck.
Here a car is negotiating the hill, known as Ratten Row, out of the village, early 1930s.

The main road into the village of Caldbeck might have been suitable for horses and carts when this picture was taken in the early twentieth century, but hardly for the volume of traffic arriving today.

Many aspects of Caldbeck have remained unchanged throughout the century, like these houses in the centre. The picture dates from about 1920.

Bowls are a favourite pastime in Caldbeck. This group was photographed on the Parish Hall Green on the Opening Day, 1905. Standing, left to right: Willie James, farmer; Jack Coulthard, farmer; Jack Ashbridge, farmer; W.H. Ivinson, grocer; William Greenup, farmer; Tom Hudson, farmer; Ted Jackson, farmer; Joe Jackson, joiner. Seated: T. Courtney, blacksmith; A. Cowley, schoolmaster; John Jennings, village squire; Jack Scott, bootmaker; Andrew Scott, odd-job man.

The post office in the centre of Caldbeck, *c.* 1930. It still occupies the same position today, although the trees on the left have been cleared to allow car parking outside the public house.

The post office in its previous position, which was next door to the present one, *c.* 1920. The Model T Ford belonged to Mr Arnison, the driver, seen here with his wife and family; they lived in Caldbeck. The entrance to the doctor's surgery used to be through the archway, and on the extreme right was the local garage.

The wheel at the bobbin mill in Caldbeck, which was reputed to be the second largest in Britain. It was taken down during the Second World War. This was also the entrance to the Howk, a pretty, wooded, riverside walk.

The brewery at Caldbeck. This is no longer in use; the buildings have been made into houses but with a similar external appearance.

Children leaving the village school in Caldbeck, early twentieth century. A modern school has now been built behind this building, which is used as an assembly hall.

The hockey team started by Miss Helen Simpson (later Lady Ewbank), daughter of the rector of Caldbeck, *c.* 1916. There is a field in the village, between the Grapes and the telephone exchange, which is still known as the hockey field. Were the long skirts a hindrance to play, and did the ball ever get lost in them?

The childhood home of John Peel, the famous foxhunter, who lived around Caldbeck all his life. His name has been perpetuated by Graves, another Caldbeck man, in the well-known hunting song 'D'ye ken John Peel', the tune of which is used as the regimental march of the Border regiment.

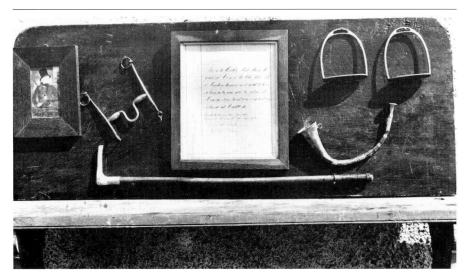

A framed photo of John Peel with the 'tools of his trade', the horse's bit, the whip, the stirrups and the horn, whose rallying call rang out over the moors far and wide.

John Peel in his top hat and grey hunting coat, whip under arm and horn in hand.

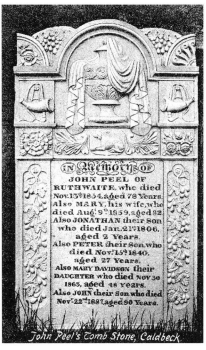

John Peel was born in 1777, died in 1854, and was buried in the churchyard in Caldbeck.

The boys have a good vantage point on the wall as the girls line up across the road at Howbeck School, Hesket Newmarket, early twentieth century.

The car attracts attention as it stops outside the Black Lion public house in Ireby, 1920s. The horse seems indifferent – or perhaps he senses future opposition.

Children coming out of school in Ireby as the horse and cart amble up the road, *c*. 1906.

A busy road in Ireby, early twentieth century. Quite an important centre for the agricultural life of the district, the village used to be self-sufficient in local shops and tradesmen.

The bulls attract attention as they are lined up at Ireby Show in 1907.

Young people of Fletchertown make the most of the snow on 21 November 1904. Coal was plentiful in this area, and the village consisted mainly of cottages for the men employed in the colliery.

Even at small stations like Mealsgate, staff were smartly dressed as they awaited the arrival of the train, *c.* 1910. This was a loop line, which connected with the Maryport to Carlisle railway.

A flock of sheep amble down the road into Mealsgate, during the peaceful period before the First World War, past the Apple Tree inn, now demolished. It's a very different scene today, as ceaseless traffic hurtles along from Carlisle to West Cumbria.

Torpenhow, a pleasant village on the south bank of the River Ellen, has not changed much over the years since 1900. Cars, vans and tractors have replaced most of the horses and carts.

Bothel, a large village, is in the parish of Torpenhow, and is at the junction of the Carlisle, Keswick and West Cumbria roads. Happily, a bypass now takes most of the traffic – a development unthought of in 1900, the date of this photograph.

SWEEPING DOWN

TO THE SOLWAY

Aspatria Agricultural College was founded in 1874 for the purpose of affording a thorough instruction in the scientific principles of agriculture and land management. It was closed in 1925. The building was demolished in 1962, and Beacon Hill School has been built on the site.

Aspatria station, *c.* 1890. The station stood on the main line from Carlisle to Maryport. You could continue down the coast to Barrow-in-Furness.

Brayton Hall, seen here in about 1880, home of the Lawson family, standing in 350 acres of parkland and a mile-and-a-half from Aspatria, was largely rebuilt in 1869. It was gutted by fire in 1918, and virtually nothing now remains.

Sir Wilfrid Lawson of Brayton Hall with a group of children, *c.* 1900.

The funeral cortège of Sir Wilfrid Lawson passes along Queen Street, Aspatria, 1906. He was a Liberal Member of Parliament for many years.

King Street, Aspatria, with the Fox and Hounds hotel on the right, pre-1914. The pinnacles on the church tower are just visible through the trees.

Schoolboys gather outside the reading room in King Street, Aspatria, built in 1894. Other children look on from Carle Terrace on the left.

When this photograph was taken in the early 1900s, children could still play safely in Lawson Street, Aspatria, without fear of being run over.

Market Square, Aspatria, with the memorial to Sir Wilfrid Lawson in the centre, 1920s. A fountain with four inlaid bronze tablets, it was designed by L. Fritz Roselieb, and built in 1908 by public subscription at a cost of £1,100. On the left of the picture is the public hall.

Horses lined up for judging at Aspatria Show, 1908.

Aspatria Volunteer Fire Brigade brass band, 1905.

A new Sentinel vehicle has just been delivered to N. Stobart & Sons at their premises in Aspatria, probably in about 1928. The works later became the Cumbrian Implement Co. Maurice Stobbart used to drive the Sentinel, and Bill Hardisty was the stoker. The Stobbarts dropped one 'b' from their trade name to save confusion with the Stoddarts.

The hearse and horse belonging to William Hastings in Outgang sawmill yard. Here, in charge of the horse, is John William Barnes, the milkman. Mr Hastings' job was the ash cart collector. When the hearse became unfit for the work he made it into a greenhouse.

Pupils at the Board School, Aspatria, on 21 September 1921. The school, on the corner of North Road and Queen Street, was knocked down some years later and a chapel built on the site.

Residents look enquiringly at the photographer in the pleasant village of Plumbland, c. 1900. The village lies on the south side of the River Ellen. A charabanc used to come once a week to take the farmers' wives to market in Maryport.

People gather in the main road in West Newton, *c.* 1910. The church, dedicated to St Matthew, was built in 1856–7, and the ecclesiastical parish was formed in November 1860.

The school in West Newton, with the west end of the church immediately to its right, *c.* 1900. It is noticeable that the girls and boys are standing in separate groups.

Allonby, 1930. On the Solway coast, Allonby has always been a popular venue for holidaymakers and day-trippers. The green on the sea front makes a good parking place.

The population of Allonby was greatly increased in the season. This bridge now carries all the main traffic from Maryport to Silloth. The beck it crosses over used to be affected by tidal flooding, but was deepened some years ago which has considerably helped the problem. In the centre is the Ship Hotel, where Charles Dickens stayed on his visit to Cumbria in 1857. This photograph dates from *c.* 1883.

The bazaar in the centre of Allonby, *c.* 1900. This was a favourite haunt of children, with an endless store of attractions on which to spend their pennies. Sadly, the shop is there no longer, and the building is now a private house.

A storm at Allonby, 25 August 1904. The high tides penetrated some of the houses near the water's edge and caused flooding when the beck, going through the village, overflowed.

Houses facing the sea at Allonby, seen here *c.* 1930, have a splendid view across the Solway to Galloway. The public news and reading room, built in 1862, is here on the left. The building is now deserted and shuttered, and the clock protruding from the tower has been taken down. The large house on the right was built in 1835 as seawater baths for the nobility, with nine changing cubicles. The money was raised in £5 shares and the plaque remains denoting many of Cumberland's eminent families which contributed. The upper floor, with balconies at the four windows, was a ballroom. Allonby was once a fashionable seaside resort for Cumberland society.

When a short trip in a charabanc was the height of excitement, Tarns Lake, just north of Allonby, was a very popular venue for an afternoon's boating or canoeing and even had a refreshment room. In a secluded corner, the lake does not have the same attraction today.

SILLOTH

ON SOLWAY

The Sunday school outing was the height of excitement for the children in a parish. Mrs

Jefferson, wife of the rector of Aikton, and her helpers dispense the contents of the picnic

hampers to the children in a sheltered corner of Silloth Green, shown here in about 1918.

With the prospect of building a dock at Silloth, the Silloth Bay Railway and Dock Company was formed and on 28 August 1856 the first train ran from Carlisle to Silloth. The station building is at the end of the lengthy platform on the right, the centre line ran down to the flour mills, and on the line on the left passengers could be taken direct to the convalescent home (see page 62).

Silloth Bay, having been a safe anchorage for ships in a storm, seemed to be the perfect place for a dock. The Marshall Dock was opened on 3 August 1859 but, as traffic increased, a new dock, with an area of six acres, was built entering through the Marshall Dock. The New Dock, seen here, was opened on 30 June 1885.

The steamer *Sugamore* berthed in Silloth Dock.

The SS *Yarrow* leaves Silloth Dock on her twice-weekly run to Douglas and Dublin. Built in 1893 especially for the route, she continued to run until 1939, having been renamed *Assaroe* in 1929, and was finally scrapped in 1947.

Almost home to Silloth *Kittiwake II* lies with a 20 degree list outside the docks. Built in 1896, she was used on the thrice-weekly Liverpool run until sold to the Dundalk and Newry SPC in 1919 – apart from some of the war years, when she had been on Government service. She was scrapped in 1928.

The SS *Yarrow* arrives at Silloth. At one time passengers used to disembark at the pier, and the arrival of the ship always attracted a great deal of attention.

The SS *Kittiwake* approaches Silloth Docks. Behind the ship the wooden pier stretches 1,000 ft seawards. A popular promenade, the lower floor of the lighthouse on the end served as a resting place while a large balloon hoisted on a pole indicated to shipping that there was sufficient water in the dock for entering. Subsidence started before the Second World War, and the promenade had to be shortened several times, finally being replaced by a timber groyne and dolphins in the 1970s.

Shipping in the New or Inner Dock at Silloth. On the left are the grain warehouses with appliances for lifting wheat and grain direct from the vessels and connected to the adjoining flour mills of Carr and Co. In the foreground the gates leading to the Marshall Dock and open sea are closed. When in this position the footbridge over the top made easy access from the town to pier, and was a fascinating walk.

The Cumberland and Westmorland Convalescent Institution was built in 1829, and is a short distance beyond the docks. Silloth being noted for its good air, it was especially beneficial for recuperation, and a special line took trains to the premises for the benefit of patients. Considerably modernized and refurbished now, it is still run by a management committee but is now known as the Silloth Hospital.

Silloth Golf Course, with its fine position above the docks and the bracing sea air, is as popular today as it was on 18 July 1907, when Haskins and Scott met there to play their one-armed match.

The Pierrots of Silloth, run by David Fuller, a well-known local singer, were a most enjoyable form of entertainment for visitors to Silloth. Dressed in white tunics and white cone hats with black pom-poms for decoration, their catchy songs would be sung around Silloth long after the show was over.

Situated in what was known as Happy Valley on Silloth Green, shelter was available for dressing-room and stage for the Pierrots, but the audience had to sit outside. Tennis courts and other sporting facilities lie beyond the spectators, while the spire of Christ Church stands out in the main street. This photograph dates from *c.* 1909.

The Queen's Hotel at Silloth overlooks the green, and has not altered much in appearance since this photo was taken in about 1921, except for the style of car that now draws up at its doors.

With a good rail connection Silloth became a very fashionable seaside resort, as is evident here in about 1910. The Solway Hotel on the right was originally called the Solway Golf but in 1904, the word golf was dropped. Like the Queen's Hotel, it became part of the Carlisle and District State Management Scheme, established during the First World War, and remained so until they sold all properties in 1972. It reopened in June 1975 and is now known as the Golf.

The open green on one side of the main street gives splendid views over the water to Criffel and the lowlands of Scotland and is famous for the beauty of the sunsets. Across the green and to the left were the baths, providing hot and cold sea water bathing for those who preferred not to go into the sea. This scene dates from the early twentieth century.

For those who enjoyed sea bathing in the early twentieth century, there was ample provision of machines and attendants for ladies, the place for gentlemen being higher up the shore. Bathing was considered safe at Silloth, but the beach was pebbly in places, and it was suggested that slippers would add materially to the comfort of the bathers.

No visit to Silloth for a child was complete without a ride on a donkey. Mr John Gray carried on a family tradition by entertaining children on the green for sixty years. Mr Gray died in 1995, but his role here stopped earlier when the green contract was put out to tender. The rides have now restarted, but in a much smaller way. Here, in the 1930s, the baths are visible behind the young riders.

South from the docks and beyond the convalescent home a gun testing station was established during the First World War, with a railway line being run out to it. Only odd traces of this important base are visible today.

In the Second World War an RAF station was built at Silloth. A runway is on the right of the picture, hangars on the left, and in the distance houses on Skinburness Road face over the sea. The station closed many years ago, and light industry occupies the hangars and part of the site, while a lido and holiday complex covers a large area in the centre of the picture.

For many years, Boys Brigade companies from around Carlisle used to converge on Silloth for their annual camp. This photograph was taken on 30 June 1904.

The East Cote lighthouse stood on open ground between the road from Silloth to Skinburness and the sea. The keeper of the lighthouse, Mr Edward Dalgleish, was ninety-two years of age when this photograph was taken. He died two years later, in 1902.

A group of workers at the Solway flour mills of Carr and Co. during the First World War.

The layout of the docks and the convenience of the large grain warehouse for the unloading of ships in the new dock is apparent. The secondary building of a similar size adjoining the warehouse, with chimney smoking, is the flour mill of Carr and Co. of Carlisle, while Criffel in the distance stands sentinel over the Solway.

The sea lashes up against the bank below houses and bungalows at Skinburness, 1920s. A continuation of Silloth, this popular residential area possesses one large hotel and some farmland to its rear. Northward from here, on land protruding into the Solway Firth, the Romans had a fort. Later, there was an active port and busy market town, which was destroyed by the sea in 1303.

A row of terrace houses and some older ones in West Silloth, 1920s. This is the area beyond Silloth on the Maryport road. These houses face towards the golf course, and a little further on there is a very large caravan and chalet park.

Section Five

THE WAVER AND
THE WAMPOOL

*The old houses in The Straits, Abbeytown, must
have been extremely small, with separate dwellings
above and below. They were pulled down early in
the twentieth century, and the road is widened now
with space behind. New bungalows face the ancient
Abbey of St Mary the Virgin, Holme Cultram,
which is visible in the background. The old house
on the extreme left still stands, but is empty and in
a state of disrepair.*

The Straits can be seen to the centre with the road leading on to the village, *c.* 1910. To the right of centre stands the Wheatsheaf inn, which still stands but is no longer a public house.

Abbeytown School with the road on to Silloth, *c.* 1912. The school still stands at the junction of the Wigton, Kirkbridge and Silloth roads, but today the playground is well fenced in to prevent children running under the wheels of vehicles.

Passengers await the arrival of the train at Abbeytown station on the Carlisle to Silloth line of the North British Railway, c. 1900. Only a short distance to the east was Abbey Junction station, where the Caledonian Railway – coming from West Cumberland – joined the North British line for a few miles before branching off for the Solway Viaduct and Scotland.

Holme Cultram Abbey, shown here in about 1910, was established in 1150 under Everard, its first abbot, as a daughter house of Melrose Abbey. It is thought that stone quarried in Dumfriesshire and brought across the Solway was included in the abbey, which was very much larger then than it is today. Years of border warfare and the dissolution of the monasteries played their part in reducing the abbey to its present size. The headstones in the foreground have been removed, and neatly cut grass gives a more uncluttered appearance.

Holme Cultram Abbey, looking towards the west door. The parishioners petitioned Cromwell at the dissolution to allow them to keep the abbey as their parish church and also as a refuge against the Scots. In 1913, the fine oak timbers were discovered beneath the plaster ceiling, some possibly twelfth-century beams. King Edward I stayed here in 1300, and again in 1307 on his way to raid Scotland. After his death at Burgh-by-Sands, his entrails were buried here, but his body was taken to Westminster Abbey. Although his father, the Earl of Carrick, is buried in the porch, Robert the Bruce, King of Scotland, was not deterred from sacking the abbey in 1319. The abbey, one of only four Cistercian abbeys to be retained as a place of worship, is still a parish church.

Newton Arlosh Church, built in 1309 by the Abbot of Holme Cultram, consisted of a nave with a western pele tower, one of the fortified border churches. It decayed in the sixteenth century, but was restored and altered in the nineteenth century. The 2 ft 7 in wide doorway into the tower is still used as the main church entrance.

A group of children outside Newton Arlosh School, *c.* 1940. The school is now closed and is a house, the children going to Kirkbride and then to Wigton Secondary Modern.

Haystacks were once a familiar sight on every farm, as pictured here in Lessonhall, *c.* 1925, but now they have been replaced by silage towers.

It is difficult to compare this tranquil scene in Waverton, near Wigton, in the early twentieth century, with the ceaseless roar of traffic going back and forth from Carlisle to Maryport and the coast today.

An early car attracts attention in Bolton Low Houses, 1920s. It gives a foretaste of the traffic to come on the main A595 road to West Cumbria. Fortunately, the village now has a bypass so it has returned to quieter days, although not as quiet as when this picture was taken.

A Conservative and Unionist garden fête at Greenhill House, 3 miles south of Wigton, then (1930s) the home of Mr and Mrs H.A. Dudding. The house has been a country house hotel for some years, and extensive conference facilities have been added recently. At this garden fête a couple entered the fancy dress parade as a bride and bridegroom. Today they could lawfully become man and wife, as the hotel was one of the first in Cumbria to be granted a licence for marriage ceremonies to be performed at it.

The Wampool bursts its banks at high tide, *c.* 1910. This view looks across from Kirkbride to Whitrigg, the houses standing in the distance. The hump in the centre is the bridge over the river, but there is no hope of reaching it until the tide ebbs.

The same scene at low tide, with children playing on the marshy ground, *c.* 1910. There was no metalled road to the bridge in those days, just a sand or dirt track depending on the weather and tides.

An engine of the Solway Junction Railway pulls its one passenger carriage and its cargo, probably of iron ore or pig iron, across the Wampool on its way to the Solway Viaduct, *c.* 1910.

A train of the North British Railway from Carlisle to Silloth crosses the river Wampool, slightly further upstream from the line to Scotland, as it nears Kirkbride, *c.* 1910.

Kirkbride Show was the highlight of the year. The residents, seen here in about 1910, gather in their finery on the showground to enjoy the attractions laid on. This event has been discontinued for some years.

A horse and cart ambles across the railway at Kirkbride station, *c.* 1904. The Caledonian Line from Scotland did not join the North British Line until west of Kirkbride, so traffic was limited on this single track, giving ample opportunity to use the crossing for pedestrians and stock.

Lessons over, children leave Kirkbride School, *c.* 1909. Built in 1876, the school continued in use until the new one was opened on 18 March 1977. This school has now been turned into a house, and the building on the left, the bacon-curing premises of Thomas and John William Crozier, grocers, has been demolished.

The north end of Kirkbride, *c.* 1910. The first house on the right has been demolished, giving more access to the road to the right, while the road in the centre leads to the church.

T.A. Gordon, grocer and baker, Kirkbride, with his first travelling shop on the road south of Kirkbride. The RAF later bordered this road and, when they relinquished the aerodrome, J.J. Porters Engineering occupied the hangar on this site. This photograph was taken in about 1910, but the family continued the business until fairly recently; it is now a private-hire bus company.

The south end of Kirkbride, *c.* 1910. The house on the right was the home of the Stormonths, who ran a large market garden there. The building on the left was the Methodist chapel, built in 1859, and closed in 1994.

The Revd William Jefferson, Rector of Kirkbride, stands in front of the rectory with his pet dog, *c.* 1910. Sadly, during a later incumbency in 1960, the rectory was burnt down and a new one now stands on the site.

The interior of the lovely little church of St Bride, Kirkbride, which stands prominently above the Wampool, *c.* 1905. Built in the Norman style, it was restored in the mid-1890s. Since then the organ has been removed to the west end.

The interior of St Andrew's Church, Aikton, *c.* 1912. The church was built in the late twelfth century in Norman and Early English styles. The very fine chancel arch is described by Nikolaus Pevsner as 'narrow Norman, the columns with scallop capitals, the arch single stepped'.

The children will have altered and left this row of cottages at The Nook, Aikton, but these houses are virtually the same as they were in about 1920, with open frontage on to the road. The transport passing by is more modern today though.

The bridal party and friends after the marriage at St Andrew's Church, Aikton, on 7 August 1912, of Mr Jonathan Hugh Strong, farmer, of Drumleaning and Miss Johnina Priscilla Todd Brown of Wiggonby. The occupation of both bride's and groom's father is described as 'Gentleman' on the marriage certificate.

A group after the marriage at St Andrew's, Aikton, on 22 June 1920, of the Revd Reginald Victor Bury of Stillington, County Durham, and Miss Emily Jefferson, daughter of the Rector of Aikton. Front row, left to right: Mr William Jefferson (bride's brother), Mrs Jefferson (bride's mother), bridegroom, bride. Back row, left to right: the Revd Canon G.E. Hasell, Miss Ellen M. Perring (bridesmaid), the Revd W. Jefferson (bride's father) and friends of the bride, including the Misses Ewbank from Boltongate.

A pleasant afternoon in the Rectory garden, *c*. 1912. From left to right: Mrs Jefferson (rector's wife), Miss Martha Mark, Royal Red Cross, Miss Emily Jefferson and Mr William Jefferson. Martha Mark, baptised on 24 May 1868, was the youngest child of William and Martha Mark of Angerton, near Kirkbride. She was a principal matron, serving for eighteen years in Queen Alexandra's Imperial Military Nursing Service, in the South African Campaign 1892–1902, and in France during the First World War, for which she received eight medals in all.

Horses were quieter than tractors and the air was free from diesel fumes in the 1920s, but it is doubtful whether any modern farmer would want to return to those days.

THE NORTHERN CORNER

The Tenor Bell makes a Request.

Relieved from duty here we sit
In well-earned ease together,
Beside the Solway's ruddy sands
Secure from wind and weather.

With near three hundred years of toil
A trifle thin our tone is,
So now at length we take our rest —
The stolen Bells of Bowness.

Yes, our voice
Grows thin.
We must cease our merry din;
We belong
To the past.
To the old and hoary past.
Never more
From the shore,
O'er the Racing Solway tide,
O'er the purple Solwayside,
Will you hear our voices calling—we
are dumb at last.

Expatriated Scots, we still
Have raised our chimes undaunted
These five times fifty years and more
Since first we were transplanted

My cousin, there, from Annandale
Was taken by the Rievers.
At Middlebie it was that I
Assembled the believers.

My friend's career was near cut short
In Dornock's icy brew.
Her iron constitution 'twas
That served to pull her through.

But still on Sunday mornings she,
With thoughts of Dornock river,
When of the "fearful pit" they sing
Can scarce restrain a shiver.

"Thou shalt not steal," the preacher said
Broad was the smile upon us.
For there we were far all to see—
The stolen Bells of Bowness.

Although, a Presbyterian bell,
I know not any "canon"
We've served Episcopalians well,
I and my friend from Annan.

Since our clamour
Must cease,
And our voices are at peace,
We now yearn
To return
To our Scottish home of yore.
Send us back,
Send us home,
I am tired of sea and foam,
Never more you'll hear us calling
by the Solway shore.

In 1648 the two bells from St Michael's Church, Bowness-on-Solway, were stolen by Scottish raiders. To lighten their load when chased, the raiders put the bells overboard. They still remain in a place called Bell Pool. Later the Bowness men rowed across and took bells from Middlebie and Dornock. Their venture succeeded and these bells were in use at Bowness, and still stand in the church, until new ones were obtained in 1905. New rectors used to receive a request for their return but the answer was always: 'When you return ours we will return yours.' Friendlier relations do exist now across the water, and the bells have been loaned to Scotland for special events and faithfully returned to Bowness.

Salmon fishing being an important part of the life of the Solway Firth, Plough Sunday always included the blessing of the haaf-net, used for fishing in North Cumbria, as well as the plough. The Revd (now Canon) Norman Joyce, Rector of St Michael's Church, Bowness-on-Solway, receives the plough from Ebdell Wills, churchwarden, while Billy Lawson waits to hand over the haaf-net for the traditional service in February 1956.

A group of local men gather at the west end of St Michael's Church, Bowness-on-Solway, possibly to lift fallen gravestones or do other work in the churchyard, c. 1910. The first man standing at the back, just visible, is Mr John Stafford, postmaster, and next is the Rector, the Revd (later Canon) L.E.D. Mitton, while the fourth along is Mr Thomas Atkinson, schoolmaster.

The interior of St Michael's Church, Bowness-on-Solway, *c.* 1910. The first known rector is recorded in 1255. Many Roman stones were used in the building of the church, which was considerably restored in 1891–2. The oil lamps, used for lighting until electricity was brought to the district in 1937, are visible here.

Thomas William Graham, son of Richard Graham, farmer, of Burgh-by-Sands, and Hannah Elizabeth Graham, daughter of John Graham, farmer, of Beck Brow, Longcroft, leave St Michael's Church, Bowness-on-Solway, after their marriage on 27 June 1939. Mrs Barbour, wife of the local policeman and a member of the church choir, is seen standing on the left.

A train approaches Bowness-on-Solway station after crossing the Solway Viaduct from Scotland, *c*. 1900. The line was opened for goods traffic in September 1869, but passengers first crossed on 8 August 1870. Fifty-one years later, on 31 August 1921, the bridge was closed to traffic as it was structurally unsafe; in 1934 it was dismantled.

The train does not appear to be imminent as people cheerfully stand on the line at Bowness-on-Solway station, the first stop in England for the travellers from Scotland, 1914. The station has been a house for some years, and the property turned into a garden and smallholding.

Fishermen of Bowness-on-Solway standing in the Solway with their haaf-nets, *c.* 1948. They stand waist deep in the swirling water, after drawing lots for their position in the line, and, holding the beam by its centre pole, hope the salmon and trout will swim into the net draped over it. Here Peter Hunter, churchwarden of St Michael's and past chairman of the parish council, 'proudly' displays his catch of a flounder.

A group of men, attired in waders and oilskins, wait to take the water with the haaf-nets at Bowness-on-Solway. From left to right: John Percival, Bob Rome, Peter Hunter, Billy Lawson, Ernest Percival, Cyril Lawson, Canon L.E.D. Mitton, Jackie Myers, Harry Jefferson and Harry Sarginson. Sadly, only John Percival, Peter Hunter and Harry Jefferson are still alive.

The Co-op sports at Bowness in 1909 attract plenty of attention. The school can be seen in the background.

Looking east in Bowness-on-Solway, the little pony and cart arrive at the post office while curious bystanders wait to see who has come. This is an early twentieth-century scene.

Looking west up the narrow cobbled street in Bowness-on-Solway, 1920s. The post office and shop were on the right, and the house adjoining was where Mr J.T. Stafford, postmaster, and his family lived. The post office is now higher up the road, and the old one has become a small private house. The cobbles have long since been made a tarmacadamed road, giving a much smoother ride through the village.

Mr R.W. Wills looks out from the garden of his house on the left while goods are delivered from the pony and cart, c. 1900. The lady in the centre is wearing a 'clootie' bonnet, a large cotton pleated cap with an additional piece to cover the back of the neck and tying under the chin. They were a much used form of head-dress in the country a century or so ago.

Perhaps the first bus to run a regular service to Bowness-on-Solway, early 1920s, with Bob Rome and Ernest Percival, who crewed it (see page 91). The old bulb horn, a means of warning, can be seen on the windscreen.

The shooting party proudly display their bag as they gather outside St Michael's rectory, Bowness-on-Solway, on 12 August 1913. The car belongs to Dr Donald. Standing, left to right: a helper and two maids, Andrew Chance, 'W.F.G.', G. Rimington, Mrs J.J. Thompson, Mr Hutton, Mr Hornby, Miss ?, Mr J.J. Thompson, Mr T. Poole and Mr W. Poole. Seated: Dr Donald, Mrs Hornby, Mrs Donald, Mrs Mitton, Eleanor C., Mrs Hutton, Greta (the dog) and the Revd L.E.D. Mitton. Paul C. Surgeon sits on the ground alongside Picknell, the other dog. Later that year there was a fire in the rectory, which caused some damage, but it was not until 1922 that it was declared unsafe, a new one built and the old one demolished.

A garden party on the lawn of St Michael's rectory, Bowness-on-Solway, in June 1936. The opener, the Honourable Mrs (later Viscountess) Anthony Lowther, on the left with Mrs Mitton, wife of the rector, surveys the proceedings while others look hopefully for bargains on the stalls.

It was obviously a great day for Bowness-on-Solway in September 1919 when Claude Lowther, Member of Parliament for North Cumberland, laid the foundation stone for the extension of the Lindow Hall. The Revd Samuel Lindow was rector of Bowness from 1889 to 1908. His successor, the Revd L.E.D. Mitton, is seated first on the left of the front row of dignitaries. The Lindow Hall was built and established under trustees in 1910.

Hazel Cruddace, now married to Dr Malcolm Smith of Whickham, Tyne and Wear, and her mother, Mrs Anna Cruddace, put finishing touches to the float in the Bowness-on-Solway carnival, *c.* 1969. The beekeeper is Robert Cruddace, and the two 'bees' in front of the hive are Ernest Taylor and Sheila Watson, now the wife of Paul Webster of Carlisle.

A group at Bowness-on-Solway School, *c.* 1951–52. Back row, left to right: Geoff Graham, Peter Wilson, William Hill, David Whitham, Allen Hodgson and Frankie Robinson. Centre row: Mavis Mossop, Tommy Martin, Joyce Bainbridge, Gordon Humes, Margaret Scott, Rita Turner, John Allen and Jenny Studholme. Front row: John Dawson, Dorothy Foster, Daphne Brough, Dorothy Pattinson, Miss McIntosh (teacher), Dorothy Pattinson, Margaret Higgleston and Bobby Sarginson. Perhaps it is not coincidence that the two girls with the same name sit either side of the teacher.

The Earl of Lonsdale, lord of the manor, built the harbour at Port Carlisle in 1819 and the first vessel sailed to Liverpool in 1825. It was quite a busy port until sailing so far up the estuary ceased with the building of the Solway Viaduct and shipping was transferred to Silloth. All that remains of the dock protrudes to the left of the house, seen here *c*. 1912. The entrance to the canal to Carlisle is visible in the centre.

The dug-out bed for the canal running along the front of Port Carlisle from the harbour continued right through to Carlisle. It was opened in 1823, and brought shipping into the city for thirty years until its conversion to a railway.

Port Carlisle, being the nearest seaside village to Carlisle, was very popular with townsfolk during the 1920s. The old harbour stands out surrounded by water, but can be reached at low tide.

All ages, from the youngest to the eldest, appear to be as interested as they are today on this important occasion when the photograph was taken at the opening of Port Carlisle bowling green bower, 29 August 1912.

The canal to Carlisle was drained in 1853, and a railway was built the following year. A small coach, called the Dandy and pulled by horse, conveyed passengers between Port Carlisle and Drumburgh, where they connected with the trains now running between Silloth and Carlisle. The last Dandy ran in 1914, and is now preserved in York Railway Museum. The horse could hardly be expected to pull the crowds gathered here, even if they had turned out for the last journey.

The Dandy arrives at Port Carlisle with driver Isaac Hickson (see next page), first on the left, in charge of the horse. It was a great excitement to children when they were allowed to sit beside him and hold the reins. First-class passengers sat inside, others on a bench outside clinging on as best they could. Farmers' wives travelled to market this way, taking the butter packed in large white wicker baskets covered with white linen cloth.

The Dandy was replaced by a small steam train, the first one leaving Port Carlisle on 6 April 1914, with the Dandy horses taken as passengers. The house in the centre used to be the harbourmaster's, while the distant land across the water is Scotland.

Driver Isaac Hickson is welcomed back to his home on the quayside at Port Carlisle by his small son, *c.* 1900.

After the little steam trains, Sentinel coaches ran on the line to Port Carlisle until the line was closed. As the last train arrives at Port Carlisle on 1 June 1932, Isaac Foster asks William Jefferson of Drumburgh – the last passenger to leave – to wait a moment to allow photographers to take photos. On Mr Jefferson's left are Mrs Lightfoot, Miss Mattocks and Mrs Martin, sadly all deceased.

As cars became more commonplace so came the necessity for petrol to be available. This photograph is from the 1940s. The post office and general store on the main street in Port Carlisle provided petrol and oil for the motorists, while the local bus time-table is affixed to the wall on the left. The post office is now transferred to the public house, and there is neither shop nor petrol in the village.

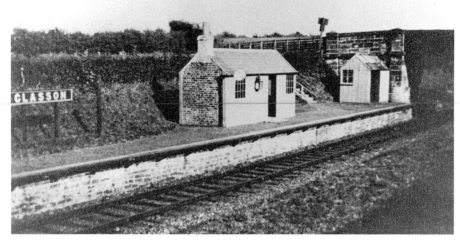

Glasson, the only station on the single-track line between Port Carlisle and Drumburgh, is now derelict and completely overgrown. The bridge on the right still carries the road into the village.

Only yards from the station, the centre of Glasson lies south of the main road from Carlisle to Bowness-on-Solway, seen here in the 1930s. On the left is the Highland Laddie public house, so named because Bonnie Prince Charlie is reputed to have last set foot on English soil when he sailed from the small jetty on the Solway's nearest point to the village.

THE ESTUARY
NARROWS

Drumburgh Castle, c. 1900. A manor house built in the early fourteenth century and enlarged and fortified in the sixteenth century, it commands a good position facing the Scottish Lowlands at the upper reaches of the Solway. Stones from the Roman wall and the small fort at Drumburgh were used in the building. The castle is reputed to be 'Fairladies' in Sir Walter Scott's novel Red Gauntlet.

Mrs Ella Coulthard, who was retiring after twenty-one years as village postmistress in Drumburgh, and Harry Salkeld, the local postman, who was moving to another district. They were photographed in a Drumburgh garden, the Solway visible in the background, on 25 September 1970, before a presentation was made to them.

Frank Henderson, on the right, surveys the high tide at Drumburgh in spring 1936, as the cyclists realize there is no possibility of going any further along the main road to Carlisle for some time.

H. Hoyle and Frank Henderson work hard to clear a path up a side road after the heavy snowfall of March 1947 in Drumburgh. A modern bungalow has replaced the farm buildings.

The general village store on the corner at the west end of Burgh-by-Sands, early 1920s. An interesting feature was the direction sign to Port Carlisle worked into the iron gate on the left. The shop has now been taken into the adjoining house, and the building on the extreme left has been demolished.

The post office in Burgh-by-Sands at the beginning of the twentieth century with Matthew Percival, postmaster from 1894 to 1914. The post office has moved to several different places since then.

The mid-fourteenth century church of St Michael, Burgh-by-Sands, was built of Roman stones from the fort on the site of which it stands. Here the body of King Edward I was laid after his death nearby before being taken to London for burial in Westminster Abbey.

The exterior of St Michael's Church, Burgh-by-Sands, showing the fortified tower, which is entered through an iron gate at the west end of the church. In the days of border warfare it was a refuge for both inhabitants and their herds.

On a bleak, windswept spot on Burgh-by-Sands marsh, within sight of the ford to cross to Scotland to wage war with Robert the Bruce, King Edward I died on 7 July 1307. The place is marked by this pillar.

The station at Burgh-by-Sands, the second stop after leaving Carlisle on the single-track line from there to Silloth.

The ferryman takes a party of young ladies across the River Eden from Rockcliffe to Sandsfield in 1928, the only means of crossing without going to the bridge at Carlisle. The fare at that time was 1*d*.

In November 1899 St Mary's Church at Rockcliffe was seriously damaged by lightning, being almost completely destroyed. It was rebuilt the following year at a cost of nearly £2,000.

Sheep shearing at a Rockcliffe farm, early twentieth century. An experienced shearer can do one sheep in approximately two to three minutes. Although professional shearers go round the country visiting farms for this purpose, some even coming over from New Zealand, many farmers do their own shearing.

The post office in Kirkandrews-on-Eden was in the house opposite the station entrance from 1901 to 1910, and was run by James Telford. The little girl seen here with her dolls' pram outside the post office, c. 1906, is Mr Telford's granddaughter. Mrs Storey, as she became, succeeded him as postmistress in 1929, continuing in the house to which he had removed in 1910, until her retirement on 30 September 1994.

The train for Silloth leaves Kirkandrews-on-Eden station, first stop from Carlisle, after putting down passengers, early 1900s. The building in the centre is the premises of Osborne's Seeds Limited. Still a family-run business, this warehouse in Kirkandrews closed in 1995.

When horses were in general use many villages had a blacksmith's forge. Here Mr Nicholson and his brother are busy shoeing a horse in their forge at Kirkandrews-on-Eden, *c.* 1940.

An important occasion at Monkhill as the villagers turn out in force in their Sunday best, before the First World War. The old mill is in the centre background.

The village of Beaumont stands on a pleasant, raised position on the south side of the River Eden. King Edward I passed through here on 4 July 1307, three days before his death on Burgh Marsh. This photograph shows Beaumont in about 1920.

Section Eight

THE EASTERN EDGES

John Johnston of Ploughlands, near Kirkbampton,

sows seed with a fiddle-drill, c. 1934.

The children of Kirkbampton School gather for a photograph outside the school, 1920s.

The choir and rector of St Peter's Church, Kirkbampton, at the main door to the church, *c.* 1952–3. Left to right: Mrs Faulder, Mrs Tyson, Mrs Ivinson, Mrs Sally Pattinson, Mrs Parker (organist), Miss Rachael Holliday, the Revd J.W. Dixon, Jennifer Ivinson, John Packard, Irene Wilson, Miss Pattinson, Betty Gillespie, Hazel Stordy and Margaret Bell.

John Mark stands by the gate of Yew Tree Farm and cottage at Kirkbampton, *c.* 1850. This was before restoration to its present condition. The Marks have lived there since the seventeenth century, the family being a customary tenant of the property which belonged to the manor of Stainton and, in 1679, purchasing the tenement when tenants were given the opportunity to do so.

Thurstonfield Lough, between Kirkbampton and Moorhouse, was a popular centre for recreation, none more so than for skating when winters were severe enough for it to freeze over. Here, *c.* 1918, Miss Emily Jefferson, daughter of the rector of Aikton, Miss Dorothy Gilbanks, daughter of the rector of Great Orton, and Miss Martha Stordy, in whose family property the Lough was situated, enjoy skating. Thurstonfield Lough is no longer very readily accessible except for those fishing by licence.

Stone House, Moorhouse, built in 1706 and presently owned by Miss Frances Wallace. It was in this house that Bonnie Prince Charles spent the night of 9 November 1745, before making his triumphant entry into Carlisle the next day.

A group at Mains Fold, Great Orton, 1910. This group of houses, which included the post office, was immediately behind the churchyard wall, and has now been demolished.

Buglers sound the Last Post at the military farewell for Richard Parker Gilbanks BA (Oxon.) at Great Orton Church. The fourth son of Canon and Mrs W.F. Gilbanks, who was rector there from 1883 till 1944, Richard Gilbanks was a Lieutenant in the Border regiment, and fell in action at Sulva Bay in 1915.

The Suffragette movement was active even in the northern parts of Cumberland. Here, in 1911, three supporters march along the main road from Carlisle to the west. With a ceaseless flow of traffic on this road today anyone walking like this would run a strong danger of being knocked down.

In the days of the Suffragettes this old car, chugging along at about 15 to 20 mph – perhaps the only one for several hours – would hardly cause a threat. This scene too is from about 1911.

Crofton Hall, a mile west of Thursby, was the stately home of the Brisco family. Portraits of that family adorn the landing walls, from which a central staircase sweeps down to the ground floor. The hall is surrounded by 140 acres of parkland, and the large ornamental lake was home to a wide variety of birds. Crofton Hall has now been demolished, and much of the parkland has been given over to agricultural use, but it is seen here looking splendid in the early twentieth century.

Passengers await a train at Crofton station, probably before the First World War, near to the main entrance to the estate and on the main Carlisle to Maryport line. Trains still run but no longer stop at this station.

The centre of Thursby village, where the main road from Carlisle forked left for the Lake District and West Cumbria and right for Wigton and Maryport, 1930s. A bypass has recently restored some tranquillity to the village, though not as much as in the days of one solitary car.

St Andrew's Church, Thursby, was built in 1846 and reputed to be on the site of a church built by David I, King of Scotland. The tower contains six bells and in the transept are five fine marble monuments to members of the Brisco family of Crofton Hall. Matty Beck Cottage still stands on the right in Matty Lonning, with the beck running opposite to it.

Thursby Show draws an expectant crowd, *c.* 1908. Shows were the high point of village life but unfortunately very few have survived to the present day.

Hope and Bendle of Carlisle were well-known wine-and-spirit merchants. Here in 1912 their flat-bed waggon, piled high with their wares, chugs along a country road west of Carlisle to make deliveries to the local inns and hostelries. One hesitates to think what would happen if a crate fell off on the rough country roads.

St Michael's Church, Dalston, c. 1912. The church stands at the north-eastern side of the village square. In red sandstone of mixed styles, it was originally built in the mid-twelfth century, and partly rebuilt in 1749 with further restoration in the nineteenth century. An attractive lych-gate has now been built over the entrance.

From the church the square at Dalston lies ahead, with the road from Carlisle to Welton and the fells passing through, seen here in the 1930s. The River Caldew, on whose banks Dalston lies, is further behind the houses on the left. A more modern version of the bus still stops there, but the square fills up with cars these days.

It would appear a perfect summer's day as spectators sit around to enjoy a ringside view at Dalston Show in 1907. This show continues to the present time as a flourishing event each August.

Rose Castle, south from Dalston, has been the home of the Bishops of Carlisle since the thirteenth century. The present castle dates from the fourteenth century, although there have been many alterations since then. On 23 June 1936 a large Diocesan garden fête was held here to raise money for the building of new churches in three towns in the diocese, where there had been large housing developments.

The state drawing-room at Rose Castle, with the hand-painted Chinese wallpaper dating from 1831. Time has not caused the striking colours to fade even though they are subject to the strong morning sunlight. Recently, however, the paper was taken off, cleaned and rehung and looks even better than before.

The village of Welton, straddling the road from Carlisle to Caldbeck before the steep ascent up Warnell Fell, *c.* 1910. The village shop was in great demand in those days, for it was only on market days that a little local bus took the farmers' wives to Carlisle or Wigton to sell the fruits of their labours and buy provisions. The Royal Oak, next to the shop, was a regular venue for the menfolk.

Children cross over the bridge, under which flows the river Caldew, in the centre of Sebergham, pre-1914. The church of St Mary the Virgin can be seen behind the house in the foreground.

The bridal party outside the home of the bride, Caldew House, Sebergham, after the wedding of Mr and Mrs John Bewley of Causa Grange, Rosley, on 25 May 1916.

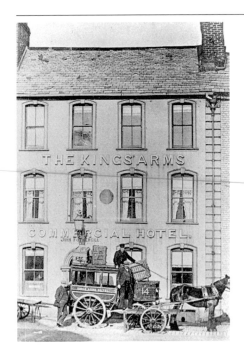

King's Arms Hotel, Market Place, Wigton, once a posting establishment where coaches changed horses between Carlisle and Whitehaven. The hotel taxi in the photo collected people from the railway station. Charles Dickens and Wilkie Collins stayed here in 1857, as described in their *Lazy Tour of Two Idle Apprentices*.

Acknowledgements

The author would like to express her very deep gratitude to everyone who has helped in any way, however small, with information towards the compilation of this book, and particularly to those who have so kindly allowed her to use their photographs.

Sue Allan • Mrs W. Bell • Carlisle Public Library
Cumbrian Newspapers Ltd, Carlisle • Mr J. Elliott • John Graham
Mr D. Hampson • Dr W.P. Honeyman • George Johnston • Miss M. Mark
Mirror Syndication International • Donald Penrice
RCHME Crown Copyright • Solway Studio
Mr J. Templeton for use of photographs from the Templeton Collection
Tullie House Museum and Art Gallery, Carlisle • Harry Wallace
Mr and Mrs R.H. Wills • Mrs B. Winter

A special thanks for his excellent photography and much assistance to Trevor Grahamslaw, without whose help this book might never have come to fruition.

BRITAIN IN OLD PHOTOGRAPHS

To order any of these titles please telephone Littlehampton Book Services on 01903 721596

ALDERNEY

Alderney: A Second Selection, *B Bonnard*

BEDFORDSHIRE

Bedfordshire at Work, *N Lutt*

BERKSHIRE

Maidenhead, *M Hayles & D Hedges*
Around Maidenhead, *M Hayles & B Hedges*
Reading, *P Southerton*
Reading: A Second Selection, *P Southerton*
Sandhurst and Crowthorne, *K Dancy*
Around Slough, *J Hunter & K Hunter*
Around Thatcham, *P Allen*
Around Windsor, *B Hedges*

BUCKINGHAMSHIRE

Buckingham and District, *R Cook*
High Wycombe, *R Goodearl*
Around Stony Stratford, *A Lambert*

CHESHIRE

Cheshire Railways, *M Hitches*
Chester, *S Nichols*

CLWYD

Clwyd Railways, *M Hitches*

CLYDESDALE

Clydesdale, *Lesmahagow Parish Historical Association*

CORNWALL

Cornish Coast, *T Bowden*
Falmouth, *P Gilson*
Lower Fal, *P Gilson*
Around Padstow, *M McCarthy*
Around Penzance, *J Holmes*
Penzance and Newlyn, *J Holmes*
Around Truro, *A Lyne*
Upper Fal, *P Gilson*

CUMBERLAND

Cockermouth and District, *J Bernard Bradbury*
Keswick and the Central Lakes, *J Marsh*
Around Penrith, *F Boyd*
Around Whitehaven, *H Fancy*

DERBYSHIRE

Derby, *D Buxton*
Around Matlock, *D Barton*

DEVON

Colyton and Seaton, *T Gosling*
Dawlish and Teignmouth, *G Gosling*
Devon Aerodromes, *K Saunders*
Exeter, *P Thomas*
Exmouth and Budleigh Salterton, *T Gosling*
From Haldon to Mid-Dartmoor, *T Hall*
Honiton and the Otter Valley, *J Yallop*
Around Kingsbridge, *K Tanner*
Around Seaton and Sidmouth, *T Gosling*
Seaton, Axminster and Lyme Regis, *T Gosling*

DORSET

Around Blandford Forum, *B Cox*
Bournemouth, *M Colman*
Bridport and the Bride Valley, *J Burrell & S Humphries*
Dorchester, *T Gosling*
Around Gillingham, *P Crocker*

DURHAM

Darlington, *G Flynn*
Darlington: A Second Selection, *G Flynn*
Durham People, *M Richardson*
Houghton-le-Spring and Hetton-le-Hole, *K Richardson*
Houghton-le-Spring and Hetton-le-Hole:
    A Second Selection, *K Richardson*
Sunderland, *S Miller & B Bell*
Teesdale, *D Coggins*
Teesdale: A Second Selection, *P Raine*
Weardale, *J Crosby*
Weardale: A Second Selection, *J Crosby*

DYFED

Aberystwyth and North Ceredigion,
    Dyfed Cultural Services Dept
Haverfordwest, *Dyfed Cultural Services Dept*
Upper Tywi Valley, *Dyfed Cultural Services Dept*

ESSEX

Around Grays, *B Evans*

GLOUCESTERSHIRE

Along the Avon from Stratford to Tewkesbury, *J Jeremiah*
Cheltenham: A Second Selection, *R Whiting*
Cheltenham at War, *P Gill*
Cirencester, *J Welsford*
Around Cirencester, *E Cuss & P Griffiths*
Forest, The, *D Mullin*
Gloucester, *J Voyce*
Around Gloucester, *A Sutton*
Gloucester: From the Walwin Collection, *J Voyce*
North Cotswolds, *D Viner*
Severn Vale, *A Sutton*
Stonehouse to Painswick, *A Sutton*
Stroud and the Five Valleys, *S Gardiner & L Padin*
Stroud and the Five Valleys: A Second Selection,
    S Gardiner & L Padin
Stroud's Golden Valley, *S Gardiner & L Padin*
Stroudwater and Thames & Severn Canals,
    E Cuss & S Gardiner
Stroudwater and Thames & Severn Canals: A Second
    Selection, *E Cuss & S Gardiner*
Tewkesbury and the Vale of Gloucester, *C Hilton*
Thornbury to Berkeley, *J Hudson*
Uley, Dursley and Cam, *A Sutton*
Wotton-under-Edge to Chipping Sodbury, *A Sutton*

GWYNEDD

Anglesey, *M Hitches*
Gwynedd Railways, *M Hitches*
Around Llandudno, *M Hitches*
Vale of Conwy, *M Hitches*

HAMPSHIRE

Gosport, *J Sadden*
Portsmouth, *P Rogers & D Francis*

HEREFORDSHIRE

Herefordshire, *A Sandford*

HERTFORDSHIRE

Barnet, *I Norrie*
Hitchin, *A Fleck*
St Albans, *S Mullins*
Stevenage, *M Appleton*

ISLE OF MAN

The Tourist Trophy, *B Snelling*

ISLE OF WIGHT

Newport, *D Parr*
Around Ryde, *D Parr*

JERSEY

Jersey: A Third Selection, *R Lemprière*

KENT

Bexley, *M Scott*
Broadstairs and St Peter's, *J Whyman*
Bromley, Keston and Hayes, *M Scott*
Canterbury: A Second Selection, *D Butler*
Chatham and Gillingham, *P MacDougall*
Chatham Dockyard, *P MacDougall*
Deal, *J Broady*
Early Broadstairs and St Peter's, *B Wootton*
East Kent at War, *D Collyer*
Eltham, *J Kennett*
Folkestone: A Second Selection, *A Taylor & E Rooney*
Goudhurst to Tenterden, *A Guilmant*
Gravesend, *R Hiscock*
Around Gravesham, *R Hiscock & D Grierson*
Herne Bay, *J Hawkins*
Lympne Airport, *D Collyer*
Maidstone, *I Hales*
Margate, *R Clements*
RAF Hawkinge, *R Humphreys*
RAF Manston, *RAF Manston History Club*
RAF Manston: A Second Selection,
    RAF Manston History Club
Ramsgate and Thanet Life, *D Perkins*
Romney Marsh, *E Carpenter*
Sandwich, *C Wanostrocht*
Around Tonbridge, *C Bell*
Tunbridge Wells, *M Rowlands & I Beavis*
Tunbridge Wells: A Second Selection,
    M Rowlands & I Beavis
Around Whitstable, *C Court*
Wingham, Adisham and Littlebourne, *M Crane*

LANCASHIRE

Around Barrow-in-Furness, *J Garbutt & J Marsh*
Blackpool, *C Rothwell*
Bury, *J Hudson*
Chorley and District, *J Smith*
Fleetwood, *C Rothwell*
Heywood, *J Hudson*
Around Kirkham, *C Rothwell*
Lancashire North of the Sands, *J Garbutt & J Marsh*
Around Lancaster, *S Ashworth*
Lytham St Anne's, *C Rothwell*
North Fylde, *C Rothwell*
Radcliffe, *J Hudson*
Rossendale, *B Moore & N Dunnachie*

LEICESTERSHIRE

Around Ashby-de-la-Zouch, *K Hillier*
Charnwood Forest, *I Keil, W Humphrey & D Wix*
Leicester, *D Burton*
Leicester: A Second Selection, *D Burton*
Melton Mowbray, *T Hickman*
Around Melton Mowbray, *T Hickman*
River Soar, *D Wix, P Shacklock & I Keil*
Rutland, *T Clough*
Vale of Belvoir, *T Hickman*
Around the Welland Valley, *S Mastoris*

LINCOLNSHIRE

Grimsby, *J Tierney*
Around Grimsby, *J Tierney*
Grimsby Docks, *J Tierney*
Lincoln, *D Cuppleditch*